INTERACTIVE **WORKBOOK**

SINGLE PARENTING SOLUTIONS™

Reducing the Risk of Child Sexual Abuse

Thank you to Nancy E. Grabe for your contribution to *Single Parenting Solutions*.

BOOKLOGIX
Alpharetta, GA

The resources contained within this book are provided for informational purposes only and should not be used to replace the specialized training and professional judgment of a healthcare or mental healthcare professional. Angela's Voice and the publisher of this work cannot be held responsible for the use of the information provided. Always consult a licensed mental health professional before making any decision regarding treatment of yourself or others.

Copyright © 2013, 2023 by Angela's Voice

Second Edition

All rights reserved. No part of this book may be reproduced or transmitted in any form or by any means, electronic or mechanical, including photocopying, recording, or any information storage and retrieval system, without permission in writing from the author.

ISBN: 978-1-61005-988-6

This ISBN is the property of BookLogix for the express purpose of sales and distribution of this title. The content of this book is the property of the copyright holder only. BookLogix does not hold any ownership of the content of this book and is not liable in any way for the materials contained within. The views and opinions expressed in this book are the property of the Author/Copyright holder, and do not necessarily reflect those of BookLogix.

∞ This paper meets the requirements of ANSI/NISO Z39.48-1992 (Permanence of Paper)

Workbook text by Nancy E. Grabe, Angela Williams.
Design and Illustration by Mark Sandlin.
Design production by Felicia Kahn.

CONTENTS

MOTIVATED TO PROTECT 1

PASSIONATE ABOUT CHANGING SOCIETAL ATTITUDES 2

DREAMING BIG 2

    DIVORCE 6

    DEATH OF A PARENT 9

    ABANDONMENT OF A PARENT/ UNKNOWN PARENT 9

    ADOPTION BY A SINGLE PARENT 10

    RISKS 10

    TIPS TO KEEP KIDS SAFE 16

    RISKS IN DATING 17

    WHAT YOUR CHILD MAY BE FEELING 20

    ROUTINES 21

    FINANCES 22

    YOUR CHILD'S PERSONAL EMOTIONS 22

    WHAT DOES YOUR FAMILY LOOK LIKE FROM THE OUTSIDE? 23

    HOW WOULD A POTENTIAL OFFENDER BEGIN 'GROOMING' A CHILD 24

    THE INTERNET HAS BECOME THE OFFENDER'S PLAYHOUSE 26

    EMOTIONAL SIGNS OF CHILD SEXUAL ABUSE 27

    PHYSICAL SIGNS OF CHILD SEXUAL ABUSE 28

    SECURING 5 AREAS 29

    YOUR CHILD 39

    WHO WILL BE WITH YOUR CHILD? 50

REFERENCES 52

    QUICK REFERENCE GUIDE FOR PARENTS 53

ANGELA'S VOICE 54

JOIN THE ANEGELA'S VOICE MOVEMENT 56

MOTIVATED TO PROTECT

Angela's Voice's goal is to expose the issue of child sexual abuse and educate adults about the risks that every child faces. It is our goal to help train adults to prepare children to respond to that risk with strong personal power and boundaries.

> **Do you know the facts about child sexual abuse?**
> - 1 in 4 girls will be sexually abused before their 18th birthday
> - 1 in 6 boys will be sexually abused before their 18th birthday
> - 70% of all sexual assaults are perpetrated against children under the age of 17
> - Currently, only 1 of every 10 sexual abuse survivors will ever tell
> - 93% of child sexual abuse cases are perpetrated by someone the child knows and trusts
> - A sex offender molests, on average, 117 children before being caught, and can molest as many as 400 children
> - There are an estimated 42,000,000 child sexual abuse survivors that need a voice in the US alone

> **Let's consider these numbers for a minute. Think of 6 people who live near you, whether you know them well or not. Write their names here:**
>
> _____   _____
>
> _____   _____
>
> _____   _____

Based on the above government statistics, provided by the Centers for Disease Control, one person from your list could be a Child Sexual Abuse survivor. And, the abuse they suffered probably would have occurred prior to the age of 17. It's a stunning reality when you begin to take a mental survey of the numbers of people that are survivors of child sexual abuse that we encounter every single day. Even more tragic is the personal and collateral damage that child sexual abuse causes in our world and that more is not being done to address this devastating problem.

PASSIONATE ABOUT CHANGING SOCIETAL ATTITUDES

Angela's Voice is working to bring about social and systemic changes in our world so our society becomes vigilant in protecting children from child sexual abuse. Several of these social changes include:

- Removing the stigma of child sexual abuse from the victims.
- Giving this epidemic public visibility
- Promoting compassion, healing, resources and programs for survivors
- Educating adults about their need to take responsibility for the protection of all children. A trained, conscientious and vigilant society puts the sex offender on notice and gives the children a circle of safety to protect them.

DREAMING BIG

Angela's Voice's dream is to create a vigilant society that will protect children from child sexual abuse. When children grow up with their emotional and physical boundaries protected, we create healthier adults. When healthier adults are raising the next generation of children, we create healthier generations.

It is our dream:
- To end this silent epidemic
- To live in a world where this plague of child sexual abuse is fully eradicated

A MOVEMENT WITH A MISSION

Angela's Voice is working hard to provide:

- Public awareness on the issue of child sexual abuse
- Prevention training to educate adults on how to predict and prevent child sexual abuse
- Aftercare healing and restoration programs into community.
- Angela's Voice is dedicated to a movement to break the silence and cycle of child sexual abuse worldwide and we invite you to be a part of this movement.

SINGLE PARENT SOLUTIONS

The purpose of this training is to provide child sexual abuse prevention education, practical tools and encouragement for the demands of today's single parent. Today, one-third of American children – a total of 15 million – are being raised without a father. Nearly five million more children live without a mother. Our emphasis is on reducing the inherent risks of child sexual abuse, which is statistically higher in single parent homes. The increased risk is not necessarily caused by single-parenthood itself, but a combination of economic pressures, family instability and conflict between parents. A single parent with adequate resources may provide a stable, nurturing home in which children thrive just as well as those who have two parents. On the other hand, a single parent who is struggling emotionally, physically, financially with little time, energy or skill for parental duties might increase a child's risk for a variety of problems. By raising your awareness of the risks, along with providing solutions for reducing them, our goal is to equip you for the safekeeping of your children. We will use the word "parent" to mean any guardian, grandparents, foster parents or other family members who are the primary caregiver of a child.

> List several factors of a single parenting household you believe contribute to the increased risk of child sexual abuse
>
> _____   _____
>
> _____   _____

Though single parenting can bring unique demands on your time, resources and finances, we at Angela's Voice believe it is possible to establish family stability and security where your child can be safe and thrive.

It would be ideal if only, every child grew up in a "Safe" world. However, we know from just watching the media that there are many dangers that our children face daily. Though we might not be able to always protect them from the dangers of the world, we can strive to keep them safe at home and give them the skills and emotional strength to face the challenges of this world. The safest possible scenario for children to grow up in, is a home where they are nurtured, valued, secure and in stable family relationships.

Before we take a look at the 'at risk' statistics for children of single parent households, we want to encourage you that you are taking the most important step in keeping your child safe. Becoming educated on the risk and ways to respond to this risk in a healthy manner are central to ensuring the safety of your children.

The 'at risk' statistics regarding children growing up in single parent households can be overwhelming. The goal in reviewing these vulnerabilities, is not to invoke fear in those raising children alone, but rather to reveal the primary areas where a child may be vulnerable. The risk factors, while glaring, do not apply to every situation and family. Our intention is not to negatively stereotype or stigmatize single parent households. A single parent household itself does not make a child more vulnerable to possible child sexual abuse, but the demands on single parents and their unique challenges can contribute to an increased risk. The most important job you have is to keep your child safe.

"It's easier to build strong children than to repair broken men."

Frederick Douglas

What does today's single parent household look like?

According to recent US Census Bureau statistics, "There are approximately 13.6 million single parents in the United States today, and those parents are responsible for raising 21.2 million children (26% of children under the age of 21)".

More than twenty five percent of today's children are being raised in single parent homes. The difficulties for these parents can be overwhelming. Some very deliberate actions are required to reduce the risk in our child's life. Deliberate parenting is required to bring the single parenting household to its optimal, in terms of stability and reduced risks.

The single parent family can no longer be classified as non-traditional based on these statistics. Single parent homes are on the rise.

Today's "traditional" family looks very different than one of 1950's America. Today:

> 1 in 2 children will live in a single parent family at some point in their childhood.
>
> 1 in 3 children will be born to unmarried parents or partners
>
> 1 in 4 children lives with only one parent
>
> 1 in 25 children lives in an environment with neither parent.
> (The State of America's Children, 1998)

As of 2007, the 'average' single parent is a mother, divorced or separated from the father. The mother heads 84% of all single parent households. She is typically employed at a rate of 79%, which usually places her outside the family home for the greater part of the day and week. She is not likely to live in poverty, though the rate for poverty is much too high, at 31% (twice that of a single father). This single mother is, on the average, 40 years old. More than half the single mothers in America are currently raising one child. These numbers show Single Parent households to be ever increasing 'common' in the world.

> How many single parent households live within a block of you or have children in school and social activities with your child?
> _____
> _____

DIVORCE

Divorce remains a common reason for single parenting. It's not unusual for children to be exposed to – or even drawn into – the conflict that happens between parents before, during and after a breakup. Some parents may pressure children to choose sides, which can leave them feeling guilty or abandoned

(Bromfield, 2008)

Lack of family stability creates additional risk factors. Single parents are more likely to move or experience other disruptions that can affect children. A parent may remarry, for example, or live with a succession of partners. Children thrive on stability. Uncertainty and emotional turmoil can increase the chance of psychological pitfalls.

Fifty percent of American children will reside in a single parent household for some portion of their adolescence. As we have come to see stability as an important factor, some questions arise.

> What does stability mean to you? To your child?
> _____
> _____
> _____

> What do you think are some ways a single parent household can provide stability?
> _____
> _____
> _____

MOMS, FOR THE SAKE OF THE CHILDREN...

Based on the fact that the mother or another female heads most single parent homes, absence of the father is a critical issue. If the father is emotionally and/or physically distant or uninvolved, our children are put at risk. The mental health of children is improved when there is an involved father.

"Overall, approximately 50% of mothers "see no value in the father's continued contact with his children... (Kelly & Wallerstein, 1980).

It becomes essential, in single mother households, to make deliberate choices for the sake of the children. According to Seltzer, J.A. "Children's Contact with Absent Parents," Journal of Marriage and Family 1988, 35% of kids living in single mother homes never see their fathers. Ten years after the breakup of a marriage, more than two-thirds of kids report not having seen their father for a year (Whitehead, 1993). More than half the kids who don't live with their father have never been in their father's house (Furstenberg & Cherlin, 1991).

FOR THE SAKE OF THE CHILDREN:

- ▶ TALK (and Listen) to children. Explain any changes that are taking place. One study showed that in only 5 percent of cases did parents explain to their children why they were divorcing or listen to their questions (Hughes, 2005).
- ▶ SHIELD kids from parental conflict. Don't ask them to take sides. Try to find a way to work with your ex-spouse.
- ▶ PAY ATTENTION to your own feelings. YOU may be burdened with guilt and self-loathing because your marriage or relationship failed. These attitudes can be contagious. If necessary, see a counselor to work through issues.
- ▶ ACCENTUATE THE POSITIVE. Children in a single-parent home often take on more responsibility, which can teach them independence. Be sure to recognize their contributions and be generous with praise.

- **WHENEVER POSSIBLE, ENCOURAGE RELATIONSHIPS BETWEEN FATHERS AND THEIR CHILDREN:** Don't speak negatively about your children's father, regardless of what you think of them or their behaviors. Every child wants their father to be their personal hero, in spite of any perceived or obvious character flaws. We all have them. The goal is to support your children's love and admiration for their father. This may require you to set aside your personal feelings, which is the job of any great parent. This does not mean you allow for unsafe visits. For unsafe parents, the relationship can be encouraged through letter writing, phone calls, which the parent can more safely control than other means of communication.

- **DETERMINE TO HAVE CHILDREN SPEND REGULAR QUALITY TIME WITH THEIR FATHERS:** Go out of your way to suggest phone calls, social activities and other interactions. Don't expect your child to do this alone. Often, a child from a single parent household will feel they are betraying the custodial parent if they want to be with the non-custodial parent. Don't enable this behavior. Let your child see, through your words and actions, you want them to have a great relationship with the non-custodial parent.

One of the worst single parenting mistakes is deciding your child does not need a continued, healthy, engaged relationship with their non-custodial parent.

> How do you encourage interaction between your child and their non-custodial parent?
> _____
> _____
> _____

"The Parental Alienation Syndrome (PAS) is a burden that a child is forced to bear when one parent fails to recognize their child's strong need to love and be loved by the other parent" (Sommer, 2004)

"Children who are exposed to the ongoing conflict and hostility of their parents suffer tremendously. The guilt they experience when their parents first separate is exacerbated by the added stress of being made to feel that their love and attachment for one parent is contingent on their abandoning the other. Although children are powerless to end the struggle between their parents, they come to believe that if they turn against one in favor of the other, the unhappiness they experience on an ongoing basis will also end.

This information applies to single fathers, grandparents and other caretakers as well. It is always best to support and help stabilize your children's relationships with their non-custodial parent/s **UNLESS DOING SO WOULD HARM THE CHILD.**

DEATH OF A PARENT

When a parent dies, there is an obvious time of grieving and feelings of abandonment. When these feelings are not processed in a healthy way, perhaps with professional help, these feelings can go on for years, leaving a child extremely vulnerable to abuse. Perhaps illness has taken a parent away emotionally or physically. In this case, a child may be burdened to care for a parent, and therefore not get their emotional needs fulfilled. In either case the void of love and nurturing from that missing parent can be exploited by a potential sex offender.

ABANDONMENT OF A PARENT/ UNKNOWN PARENT

When a child does not know or have a relationship with a parent, it imprints a huge question, "Why didn't they love me? Why did they leave me?" This confusion and relationship void causes the child to continuously search for love and acceptance. When a child feels abandoned they seek love and acceptance. When a potential abuser realizes the child's insecurities, this too can increase the risk of a child being sexual abused.

Parents without mates sometimes lean on children for support during lonely periods. Children are naturally protective of their parents, but asking them to solve adult problems can cause them to stifle their own feelings and feel overwhelmed. Never discuss adult problems or money issues with young children. Talk about their feelings, not your fears. Make sure they have time to act like kids. (Bourland, 2000/2001).

ADOPTION BY A SINGLE PARENT

Many single parents adopt children privately or from the U.S. foster care system, as well as from other countries. Though historically not an acceptable practice, single parent adoptions have increased over the past two decades. National statistics are not available for confidentiality reasons, but the National Adoption Center says that one-third of its adoptions are by single parents, and while most are women, the number of men adopting solo is growing. The greatest population of children adopted into single parent homes is older children and those with special needs. These children have inherent struggles that may increase their vulnerability to be sexually abused. Adoptive parents need to be even more sensitive that an adoptive child, may have experienced previous trauma. The greatest need that these children have is the need for love and acceptance.

Whatever the reason for the absent parent situation, children tend to develop the belief that they, personally have been rejected, that they are unwanted or unlovable. These beliefs make them prime targets for offenders of Child Sexual Abuse. As their parent, we need to allow our children to discuss these feelings. It is healing to have someone validate your fears and offer compassion. If their feelings are extremely intense or do not subside after several talks, it may be time to consider professional counseling with someone skilled in this area. Our children need all the strength we can instill in them, and they need to know that we will always listen, especially to their innermost feelings.

RISKS

Children from single parent households are at greater risk.

From one research study to another, the statistics regarding the risks for children raised in single parent households remain similar, yet one thing they don't all agree on is why. There is much debate on the underlying causes from income variables, time children spend away from the custodial parent, parental distractions from increased responsibilities. Regardless of why, it's important examine these risks, so single parents have a clear idea of the necessary steps to reduce the likelihood of your child becoming one of the statistics.

- ☐ **Depression** is 3 times higher than children raised by two biological parents
- ☐ **Substandard health** often arising from stress and unresolved emotional conflict
- ☐ **Emotional stress** contributing to reductions in healthy physical and emotional well-being as well as relationships and self-esteem
- ☐ **Difficulties in school** grades, behavior, drop-out rates
- ☐ **Raised in poverty** this number is 26% higher than for children raised in the home with both parents
- ☐ **Greater and earlier** sexual activity
- ☐ **Teenage pregnancies**: 75% come from single parent homes
- ☐ **Criminal activity**: children of single parent homes account for more than half of all youths incarcerated for criminal acts
- ☐ **Violent behavior**: 11 times more likely to exhibit violent behavior than a child from a two parent household
- ☐ **Gang recruitment (a powerful lure)**: The loss of family identity, along with such factors as loneliness, isolation, detachment, etc. provide a powerful magnetic force, drawing children into gangs
- ☐ **Murderers**: 72% of teenage murderers are from single parent households
- ☐ **Rapists**: 60% of rapists, in any age bracket, who have committed rape, come from single parent households
- ☐ **Chemical dependency**: children raised without both parents account for 75% of children in chemical dependency hospitals
- ☐ **Suicides**: 63% of all suicides are individuals from single parent households

Has one or more of your children struggled with any of the above behaviors? If so, check which ones?

Go back and place a checkmark in the box next to any risk category one or more of your children have experienced.

In the US Department of Justice study, "Child Sexual Abuse Victims and Their Treatment", researchers noted that "a study of 156 victims of child sexual abuse found that the majority of the children came from disrupted or single-parent homes; only 31 percent of the children lived with both biological parents. Although stepfamilies make up only about 10% of all families, 27% of the abused children lived with either a stepfather or the mother's boyfriend."

Nearly 70% of the child sexual abuse victims in this study came from single parent homes.

This is one of the alarming risks of raising children without both biological parents and may be an underlying cause of many of the other risky behaviors previously mentioned. We will address key components for why these rates increase in the single parent household, along with strategies for minimizing them.

THE STARK REALITY OF WHY CHILD SEXUAL ABUSE RATES INCREASE IN SINGLE PARENT HOUSEHOLDS

For the single parent, there is increased responsibility and decreased time. This can also be the case in families dealing with loss and transition, such as illness, trauma, or some other life altering dilemma. In each case, children are put in new and more unstable situations, increasing many of the risks, especially child sexual abuse.

This new environment brings three key components:

- Children are less likely to be supervised by a parent
- Children are less likely to have their actions monitored, in and outside the home
- Children are less likely to have meaningful communication with their parent(s)

How much time does your child(ren) spend unsupervised each day? _____

How much time does your child spend engaged in activities you do not monitor personally each day? _____

How much time do you spend in meaningful communication with your child each day?
_____

Though it may appear that being part of a single-parent household always indicates a negative family environment, many single-parent families find a balance and successfully thrive in today's world!

Healthy adjustments will need to be made in order to keep children safe and secure.

HOW YOU, THE SINGLE PARENT, MAY BE VULNERABLE

Single parenting, by nature, denotes increased responsibilities and decreased time. These two facts suggest a certain built-in vulnerability. One of the most likely outcomes is distraction. You may be distracted from your child's needs as you focus on other household management issues. Work, bills, extra-curricular activities, and relational stresses outside the home can consume valuable time and remove attention away from your child. You may find yourself somewhat disengaged from your child, and their emotional needs.

> List 6 things that take your attention away from your child when you're together. Things like phone calls, email, adult conversation, worries, mental/physical fatigue, or stress.
>
> 1. _____ 2. _____
>
> 3. _____ 4. _____
>
> 5. _____ 6. _____

Let's try an activity:

If you are in a group...

Have one person hold a piece of paper with the words: "Self-esteem" written in the center of it. Have them walk up to each member of the group, one at a time, acting excited like a child with something to share. They will say: "Look what I did today". Have each member of the group in turn say: "Not now, I am ...!" fill in the blank with whatever they might be doing (watching TV, making dinner, paying bills, having adult time...). Having said "not now" they will rip off a piece of the paper marked Self-esteem and hand it back to the "child".

If you are alone... (do it even if it feels silly)

Take a piece of paper and write "self-esteem" in the middle of it. Then think of all of the responses the adults in your child(ren)'s life might give them that say "not now". As you think of them rip off a piece of the paper.

When you are done: Think of all the caretaking adults in your child(ren)'s life that do this: babysitters, aunts, uncles, grandparents and yourself. Then look at what is left of the child's "self-esteem" after bits and pieces have been ripped off. How does that feel to have had small pieces of your self-esteem ripped away?

Remember: Sex offenders are looking for children with low self-esteem.

Low self-esteem is a risk factor for victimization by others" (Emler, 2002). So remember it is ok to ask a child to wait, but be sure that you remember to give them the attention that they were asking for. One great technique for this is First – Then. First... let me finish this... Then... I will look at that. Be sure to follow through with the "then" or it will mean nothing!

> List some other ways to be sure to build your child(ren)'s self-esteem.
>
> _____   _____
>
> _____   _____
>
> _____   _____

Due to the pressures and demands outside your home, the need for child care often arises. A single parent may be receptive to any offers for help to fill this void. Free help may be considered a blessing, potentially causing one to disregard the usual safety concerns for the sake of getting quick and affordable help. This presents a situation sex offenders look for, where they can insert themselves easily into the life of a single parent and his/her children. Be on guard for anyone offering to relieve you of your parental responsibilities, even for short periods of time.

Be aware of the possibility of a juvenile babysitters acting out on your child sexually. The rise in teen exposure to pornography can create curiosity. Juveniles that have experienced sexual abuse themselves may act it out again with younger children. Please do not be afraid, just vigilant. When using a new sitter, try to use them for short times and see how your kids feel about them before using them for prolonged absences. Utilize dropping in to set an expectation that you could return anytime unexpectedly.

Have you ever had a juvenile or adult care for your child whom you know little to nothing about? _____

_____

How often? _____

_____

Another area to consider is inserting a new adult role model into the life of your child. Often, a single parent looks to fill the void left by the absent parent, hoping to meet some of the emotional needs of the child. While this may seem like a good idea, there is no one who can fill the role of the other parent. And, encouraging your child to spend time alone – one adult to one child – with a family member, community leader, teacher, or neighbor can lead to danger.

TIPS TO KEEP KIDS **SAFE**

1. Teach your children the buddy system. When your children go outside or somewhere without you, encourage them to stay with a buddy. Sibling or friends make a great buddy. Sex offenders need to get your child alone.
2. Have an open door policy. When your child is with another adult or teen they need to have their door open. This way you can hear and see what they are doing. Sex offenders are looking for privacy.
3. Have a Drop in Policy. You do not have to tell your kids or the caregiver. You do need to stop in unexpectedly. You might come home earlier than you said you would. You might stop by the house to get something and leave again. You want any potential sex offender questioning, "Will they be home soon or drop in on us?" You can also have a friend stop in to check on your child and caregiver. You can leave something for your friend to pick up, so that there is an expectation someone will be stopping by.
4. Talk with your Child and really listen! Ask what your child did while you were gone? Watch for any uncomfortable reaction. If a child is uncomfortable with a caregiver, ask lots of questions. Children need to believe that we are going to listen to them. A good rule is to ask 5 questions before you react. You may really need this caregiver, but if you shut your child down you may miss the information that they are not safe. What questions should you ask? Don't ask 'why'; everyone feels a 'why' as judgmental. Instead ask for an example: You say you don't like her; tell me something she did that you didn't like. Ask how they make your child "feel". You might even ask if you should recommend this caregiver to other people. Then listen; don't tell them their feelings are wrong. Acknowledge their feelings; this does not mean you agree. It does mean that you hear what they are saying. Then evaluate if this person is worth the risk.
5. Give them a NO RUN TELL Plan of Protection:
    a. Scream "NO" when touched inappropriately
    b. RUN away from the person immediately
    c. TELL and tell until someone believes you.

Give your child a plan of what to do, who to call, where to run if faced with a dangerous situation. For children too young to flee, consider monitoring technology and let your caregiver know that their actions are being monitored. This may reduce risky behavior.

RISKS IN DATING

A word about Dating: The introduction of dating brings up a myriad of potential challenges for you and your child. There can be an increase in emotional tension, fears and jealousy, as your child faces the prospect of what they may see as a 'replacement' of their non-custodial or absent parent. Aside from this, the most significant danger is simply bringing yet one more unknown adult into the life of your child. It is wise to take things slowly. It is a good idea to keep initial dating activity outside your home and family. A good rule is don't introduce your children to a date until, such time you know the person well and are sure that you will date them for a good while longer. Too many changing dating relationships can confuse and worry children. Once you feel comfortable with the relationship between just the two of you, then slowly introduce them to your child(ren).

It never hurts to vet your dating partner. Ask to speak to the person who they were last closely involved? Ask how they perceived interaction with their children. Ask if they were ever uncomfortable or if boundaries were ever compromised?

Here are some questions to ask yourself or discuss with a friend:

> Do you allow a first date to come to your home when your child is there? _____
> _____
> How long do you need to know a date before you invite them to spend time with your family? _____
> How long do you need to know your date before you allow them to be alone and unsupervised with your child(ren)? _____
> Have you talked to others in your dating partner's life about their interactions with children? _____

Remember the same rules that apply to Caregivers are good for Dates too.

Sometimes children feel there are being replaced by a new 'love' in your life. They may go looking to be loved somewhere else, unless it is safe to talk to you. What can you do? Keep family traditions alive. This lets children know that the new person is not changing everything. Remember to plan some special one on one time without your date to let your child know they are not replaceable. Dating is a balancing act that is best done with your child's input. Do not give up your status as parent or adult, but do allow your child to speak openly with you about their feeling for and about your date. Do your best not to overreact. Thank your child for sharing their feelings, even if you don't like them. Slow down your relationship if you need to let your child get more comfortable. Just knowing you care how they feel, makes your child secure and more likely to tell you if anyone is inappropriate with them.

YOUR CHILD'S HOPE RESTS WITH YOU

As a single parent, you have to manage your time and attention to best support security and stability within your family. It's critical to meet your own needs so you are at your best to meet your child(ren)'s. Many single parents, without realizing, turn to their adolescent child to get these needs met. It is critical to keep a watchful eye on your child's exposure to adult matters like finances, emotions, self-esteem challenges, relationship problems and the like. They are not mature enough to handle the responsibility. You must make a diligent effort to fulfill these needs outside your parent-child role.

> ▸ Develop strong emotional support networks through parenting groups, counseling and houses of faith. Close personal friends can be a great source as well. In times of increased demands and stress, it becomes critical to reach out for help. No man or woman is an island. Remember, the goal is to be the best YOU so you can be your best for your children.

Name 4 friends, mentors, counselors or family members whom you could call on for emotional support any time of the day or night.

1. _____

2. _____

3. _____

4. _____

▸ Work on improving your self-esteem. Read books, listen to CD's, and seek counseling if necessary. Life can bring any number of challenges to one's self-image. Setting aside time to remind yourself of your strengths can put things back in perspective.

▸ Make sure you set aside time for friendships, social connection and de-stressing. Everyone needs connection. As a single parent, these relationships afford you the opportunity to step away from your role as caretaker and unwind. You'll have to make an effort to meet this need. If you have fewer friendships than you'd like, join a social club, an athletic venture, art class, or many of the other great social functions available today.

List several ways you allow yourself to connect with adult friends or social networks every month.

_____   _____

_____   _____

▸ Do things for yourself that give you a sense of accomplishment and fulfillment. For many, this can be your work or volunteer opportunities. For others, it may be sports involvement, creative writing, or simply setting personal short term and long term goals. Whatever the case, discover what rewards you emotionally and engage. You and your family will be better for it. This can be a great family activity.

List a few of your favorite activities, in terms of emotional fulfillment. These would be things that fuel your passion and make you feel good about yourself.

_____   _____

_____   _____

Every home has a particular emotional climate. It's important to assess yours, looking for strengths to build on and weaknesses to stabilize.

Whether your child was born into a single parent home, adopted by you as a single parent, experienced a divorce, death or other transition, there is a particular emotional climate they experience. Any instability in this emotional climate contributes to a unique vulnerability for your child.

A potential sex offender easily spots this vulnerability.

Though your child may have always been raised in a stable single parent home, experiencing no sudden or significant change, taking a look at the following dynamics may help you identify areas where you can improve your parent-child relationships.

LET'S LOOK AT WHAT YOUR CHILD MAY BE FEELING INSIDE THEIR SINGLE PARENT HOUSEHOLD

Relational Dynamics among family members

Whether your single parent home is recent or long-standing, your child may be feeling some of the following:

- Isolation or silence, closing off or diminishing prior forms of communications between family members
- Stress or worry, making the home an insecure and frightening place for your child
- Chronic distractions and/or emotional discontent

Your child's emotional needs may be short-changed because you are focused on the demands of single parenting or other family transition. The potential animosity of family members and parent(s), or emotional neglect, may be damaging to your child. If you have become a single parent home because of a death, be sure you and your children have and are receiving the care you need to heal. Children will often feel abandoned by the deceased parent, even though as adults we can see this was not intentional.

The incarceration of a parent can also make a child question their worth. Open discussions can do a great deal to alleviate these thoughts. Helping your child see that adults make choices for themselves that have nothing to do with other people can help your children manage these thoughts. This is also a great lesson that there are always consequences to bad decisions.

ROUTINES

Family routines are vital. Routines such as family meals, bedtime and family celebrations can create a safe feeling of belonging. If we let these activities become mechanical or non-existent, they can lead to your child feeling a sense of isolation, conflict and insecurity. Simple routines like meals, a weekly game night or bedtime rituals can make all the difference in a child's sense of security and self-worth. These routine activities are also vital opportunities for open and intimate conversations that will allow your child the opportunity to discuss anything that is troubling them. Additionally, this focused attention on your child allows you the time to discover any changes in attitude or behavior.

Do not make the mistake of believing the activities need to be big or expensive. Something as simple as a game night or camping in the living room in a homemade tent can be meaningful. Belonging is one of the greatest protections we can give our children, take a minute to list 2 simple things you can or will do on a regular basis with your child or children.

1._____

2._____

What day and time of the week can you set aside for these activities?

_____

Hint: If you are having troubles thinking of things, think of things you enjoyed. Activities you wished your family had done or things you have seen or heard others have done. You don't have to be overly creative.

FINANCES

The family finances can change abruptly in a single family home. Whether it is due the loss of a job, the parent partner or ongoing challenges with a single parent income, these changes make life difficult for everyone. When pressures arise in finances your child can feel the stress. Activities and perks once available to your children may be eliminated or reduced due to tighter budgeting requirements. The loss of fun events, sporting activities and family outings along with 'extras' inside the home can be a source of disappointment, grief for your child. And your stress can bleed into your child's life.

Having a budget and sticking to it can help with the stress. Research repeatedly shows that quality time is most important. Children of the rich are not happier or more balanced because of the "things" they are given or places they are taken. There is no substitute for personal time and attention. Remember spending time doing errands or chores together help children learn life skills, gain a work ethic, and feel valued and appreciated. All of these things protect them from dangers that life can bring their way.

If an adult takes interest in your child wanting to provide material things, trips, outings you may be relieved and want them to take advantage of opportunities you can't provide. This is a motive used by sex offenders and you need to be aware. Make sure your child understands that no one should require them to do anything in exchange for these privileges.

YOUR CHILD'S PERSONAL EMOTIONS

- ▶ Shock or trauma (if experiencing a separation, divorce, or death of a parent)
- ▶ Internalizing the blame for any perceived lack or dysfunction, thinking they should be able to fix the problem. This is one of the most common reactions by children. It would be wise to address this possibility throughout the challenges of life and family.
- ▶ Grief or loss is best understood as the difference between what we want, hope for or expect and what happens. Given this definition your child, even a child that has never had a second parent, may struggle when "everyone" else has that second parent. Remember not to judge or justify; just listen to their disappointment

and comfort them. Saying things like, "I am so sorry, I know it hurts" or "I think I would feel like that too" or "I felt like that when I was your age" can really help. You are not agreeing; just validating their feelings. This is the first step to healing.

DEMANDS OUTSIDE THE HOME: MORE?

- For the single parent, adult demands outside the home can be great, leaving your child with new and varied caregivers. Doing so can lead your child to elevated feelings of isolation and emotional separation. When facing new caregivers who may not be adequately qualified, emotionally healthy or even safe, your child's security and stability is at greater risk.

WHAT DOES YOUR FAMILY LOOK LIKE FROM THE OUTSIDE?

Is a potential sex offender watching? What would he or she see?

A sex offender will look for challenged home environments where the child may be vulnerable to 'grooming.'

Grooming is a process by which the sex offender inserts him or herself into the life of a child, for the ultimate purpose of sexual violation of the child.

In order to identify potential victims, the sex offender looks for

- Single parent homes
- Unstable family relationships
- Recent loss or trauma
- A child spending large amounts of time alone or unsupervised
- A child with a 'loner' personality (one who isolates)
- A child with emotional, educational or behavioral problems.

- A child with special needs that is mentally, physically or emotionally challenged.
- A child with low self esteem
- This list is by no means exhaustive.

HOW WOULD A POTENTIAL OFFENDER BEGIN 'GROOMING' A CHILD?

A sex offender is on the lookout for opportune changes in the life of a child and his or her family. This person will begin to engage a child and family, attempting to build credibility and trust. He or she will look and act like an interested and concerned individual, often times offering to fill in where either parent is unavailable. The potential sex offender may offer to provide child care, handyman services, friendship, mentoring, athletic coaching, tutoring or other support in an attempt to become part of the inner circle of a child and his or her family. A single parent with little support may find someone like this to be indispensable. That alone is cause to stop and question, but not for fear.

This process of 'grooming' can take months, even years, before a potential sex offender actually begins to make sexual contact with a child. For most, they see no 'red flags' from adults in the life of the child they seek to manipulate. It's an insidious and calculated plot to betray the trust and innocence of their victims. You can reduce or eliminate the risk by asking questions of yourself – critical questions regarding any juvenile or adult involved in the lives of your family and children, including extended family members.

Do you have anyone in your life or the life of your child who has become indispensable?
_____

Is there someone that has shown a considerable interest in you and your child or children? _____

Is there anyone who desires to spend quality alone time with your child or children?
_____

Is your child willing and able to talk about what they do alone with this person?
_____

> How does this juvenile or adult react to you showing up unannounced? _____
>
> Does your child's personality change when they are going to spend time with this person? _____
>
> Have you talked to your child about appropriate touch? _____
>
> Does your child feel like they can tell you anything and you will believe them?
> _____

Remember a background check only works if the sex offender has been caught; many sex offenders have not yet been caught, nor offenses reported to law enforcement. Even if there is a report filed, prosecution is challenging because of delayed disclosure, credibility of the child's disclosure and lack of physical or forensic evidence.

We need to and want to believe our children. Unfortunately, they often give us reasons to question them. Some kids love to exaggerate, embellish, don't tell the truth, or entire truth, to the point you always wonder if they are telling the truth. Then when our child accuses an adult of sexual abuse, we worry that believing them will destroy the life and reputation of this helpful adult or juvenile.

Let's look at the statistics on false allegations of sexual abuse. In a study done by the Denver Department of Social Services in 2000; they found that after removing reports where an adult has coerced their child to falsely report only 1.5% of all reports were false (Oates, et al., 2000). In 1999, the U.S. Department of Health and Human Services, Administration for Children and Families, Children's Bureau looked at four different states (Florida, Missouri, Vermont, and Virginia) reviewing Child Protective Service (CPS) records to determine the extent of false reporting. This review showed that intentionally false reports comprise less than 1% of all unsubstantiated reports of child abuse (0.00999634 or less than 1 out of 100 unsubstantiated reports). Regardless of the study reviewed, the statistics were never above 14% for false reporting. These higher percentages always included children who had been coerced into reporting by a caregiver and children who had been coerced by a relative to recant because of the damage the report would do to the family.

Our children need us to believe them! If only 1 to 2 children will falsely accuse in every 100 reports, they deserve our faith and trust in them. When our young children have knowledge of sexual behaviors beyond their years, it is a good indication something inappropriate is happening. We need our children to have faith that as their only parent, they can count on us to believe and protect them.

THE INTERNET HAS BECOME THE OFFENDER'S PLAYHOUSE

According to the Crimes Against Children Research Center, "1 in 5 US teenagers who regularly log on to the Internet say they have received an unwanted sexual solicitation. Solicitations were defined as requests to engage in sexual activities or sexual talk, or to give personal sexual information."

With the rise in Internet social networking (Facebook, Twitter, TikTok, Instagram, etc.), gaming, on-demand services for movies; coupled with the increased ownership of smart phones and other electronic devices, there is a significantly higher risk for your child to be exposed to an online sex offender. Internet 'grooming' is similar to in-person grooming but with complete anonymity. The 13 year old girl your child is 'friends' with online, may actually be a 50 year old man who lives up the street or three states away. His intention may be to glean enough information and emotional ties with your child as to lure them into an offline sexual relationship.

Today's advances in technology, software capabilities and GPS (location services) have nearly everything we do connected to databases housed on the Internet. Many sites continue to reduce one's ability to secure information, photos and outsider access. Because of the increase in access and decrease in security, these devices and technologies have become a haven for potential sex offenders.

Do you have parental controls installed on your child's computer? _____

Do you allow your child's computer or other internet access (via phone, etc.) without you present? _____

Do you have the computer and site passwords for all the places your child accesses the Internet? _____

Do you regularly check your child's phone, text and social networking messages and friends? _____

Your best defense against online sex offender access to your child is training and vigilance. Every parent needs to be trained on Internet safety: how to block, secure and monitor your child's internet and electronics' activity.

"Only one-third of households with Internet access are actively protecting their children with filtering or blocking software," according to the 2006 report from the National Center for Missing and Exploited Children

ENGAGED PARENTING IS THE KEY TO CHILD SAFETY

For more information on sex offender 'grooming' and internet safety, refer to the following resources:

The Grooming Mystery: Unmasking the Sex Offender
Internet Safety 101 (produced by Enough is Enough)

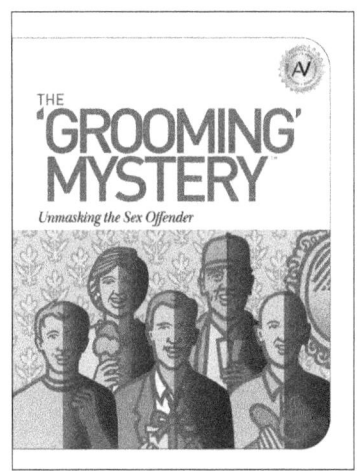 

Let's take a look at a few of the potential signs of child sexual abuse.

Any change in your child's normal behavior should be carefully monitored. It's important to talk with your child and listen to what they're telling you. Many of the signs will not be uncovered by communication, so pay attention to behavioral signs and a distinct unexplainable change in behavior.

EMOTIONAL SIGNS OF CHILD SEXUAL ABUSE ARE:

- ☐ **Keen awareness of adult issues**: A child may suddenly seem to know more about sex than is age appropriate, use sexual language and act out sexually. Consider this a clue that there may be some outside exposure to sexual content or behavior.
- ☐ **Withdrawal**: Though some withdrawal will come as your child matures, any sudden or long-term sign of it needs to be viewed with concern.
- ☐ **Depression**: It has many manifestations and parents would do well to learn more about it. The overall feeling that a child does not have interest in things that used to bring them joy is a concern.

- ☐ **Acting out**: This would be the more aggressive or outward signs that a child is experiencing emotional instability. Keep an eye out for verbal combativeness, risky behaviors, fighting, etc.

- ☐ **Lying**: A child who is lying is a child who is hiding something. It would be best to engage in conversation to find the underlying cause. Some will lie out of fear they aren't perfect when a parent's expectations are too high. Others will lie because they are involved in behavior or activity they clearly know is unacceptable.

- ☐ **Sense of hiding something**: Most parents know when their child is hiding something from them, whether it be a secret, a fear, a feeling they don't feel safe to share.

PHYSICAL SIGNS OF CHILD SEXUAL ABUSE ARE:

- ☐ **Lack of concentration**: When a child, or adult for that matter, cannot seem to concentrate or remember details, it can be sign of severe emotional and physical distress.

- ☐ **Bed wetting**: This is often, but not always, associated with child sexual abuse. Intervention by a doctor is recommended.

- ☐ **Genital redness and irritation**: Again, this is often, but not always, associated with child sexual abuse. Intervention by a doctor is recommended.

- ☐ **Urinary tract or yeast infections**: Though this can arise from lack of good hygiene and high sugar diets, it's best to investigate the source. Intervention by a doctor is recommended.

- ☐ **Non-suicidal self-harming (cutting, burning, pulling hair)**: Any sign of these behaviors is a clear red flag and should be dealt with immediately. Seeking professional counseling and medical help is recommended for any of the above emotional or physical signs of distress.

Caution: There could be no discernible signs a child is being sexually abused!

Please check any of the above symptoms you have witnessed in one or more of your children.

SECURING 5 AREAS

We are focusing on SECURING 5 AREAS:

- Home
- Internet and Electronics
- School
- Neighborhood and
- Community

We have 2 PRIMARY GROUPS OF PEOPLE CONCERNS:

YOUR CHILD

- Their sense of value
- Trusting their inner voice
- Equipping them to THRIVE

OTHER People in your child's life

- Are they safe?

1: SECURITY AT HOME

Basic DWELLING SECURITY may seem obvious, but it's important to cover. You and your child need to feel more safe at home than in any other environment, emotionally (which we'll cover later) and physically. In today's world, it becomes more important to secure homes from unwanted intruders. We encourage wisdom and caution, not fear.

Securing your home means having locks on outer doors, fence gates, garage entries, etc. Set guidelines with your children about when and how these entries need to be locked. Law enforcement recommends all doors be locked and garage doors be closed at all times, unless coming in and out frequently.

INTERACTION SECURITY with family, friends, neighbors and other visitors can bring a different set of challenges. You and your child need an established set of guidelines. Always 'know' who is in your house, on your property or within close range. Be aware of your surroundings, taking note of strange behaviors or onlookers.

We believe no child should answer a door or phone if they are home alone.

Children need to be taught what to do if someone comes to the door when you are not home or available:

> Is it ok for them to open a door to someone they don't know? _____
>
> At what age? _____ Does an adult need to be present in the house for them to do so?
>
> What should they say to an adult at the door if you are not home? _____
>
> What phone rules do you have? _____
>
> Is it ok for them to answer the phone from an unrecognized number? _____
>
> At what age? _____
>
> What about numbers they do not recognize? _____
>
> What is your child allowed to say to someone on the phone or at the door? _____
>
> Are they allowed to tell people they might be alone and unsupervised? _____

Basic EMERGENCY SECURITY establishes a much needed plan of safety in the unlikely event of a home emergency. It's critical to map out a plan for these scenarios, instruct your family and role play from time to time. You'll need an emergency plan for the family and another one if your child spends time in the home alone. This would include the addition of where and whom to seek help from, when you aren't with them.

> Things to consider in an emergency plan are:
>
> ▶ Fire, flood, carbon monoxide, gas leak, etc. – where extinguishers are, how to leave various parts of the home, depending on where one might start, purchasing escape ladders for upstairs rooms.
>
> ▶ Intruder entry – where to meet or hide in the home, how to escape the home to run for safety, where to go and who to contact if this happens.
>
> ▶ An unsafe caretaker or family member violates your child's boundaries – how to escape the caretaker or family member, who to tell, and how to reach safety.

We cannot stress enough how important it is to write these plans down, post them in public view for the family, talk about and rehearse them with each member of your family.

Have you ever written a home emergency plan for your family? _____
_____

Your child learns best when you model secure behavior in front of them. Start in the home.

Your local fire department and police department may have community support to help you make your plan, give them a call.

2: SECURE INTERNET AND ELECTRONIC DEVICES

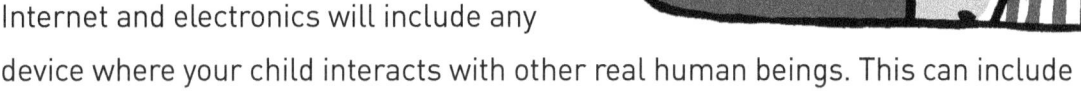

Internet and electronics will include any device where your child interacts with other real human beings. This can include

- email
- tablets
- gaming devices
- social networking sites
- Cell phone calls, texting and web access

Internet and cyber safety experts agree, close monitoring is essential to keep children safe online.

SET FIRM GUIDELINES FOR YOUR CHILD:

Only allow internet and electronic usage in public areas of your home, under your watchful eye. Children of any age should not be allowed private and unmonitored access to these devices. Be mindful of other locations your child might visit and what is allowed there.

Equip any and all computers and electronic devices with parental monitoring software to regularly monitor Internet search history and sites visited. These programs will tell you when, where and how long your child is accessing the web. Some monitoring will need to take place the old fashion way, by picking up your child's phone and checking their call and text history.

Know and monitor ALL passwords required for entry to internet and electronics. If a device allows a password, you need to know. If your child accesses a devise without your permission, we advise you to protect your passwords and allow access based on your rules. Your child would not be able to access devices without you logging in a protected password.

Know their Internet, phone, text and gaming 'friends' and how your child knows them. Insist this circle of 'friends' be limited only to individuals you each know personally. The wider the audience the less security.

Keep the lines of communication open, questioning your child about their Internet and electronic activity. Ask them if they meet face to face with anyone they know only from the Internet. Be careful to not overreact or they will keep secrets.

Decide in advance, with your child, what types of personal information and photographs they will be allowed to post.

Prohibit unsupervised use of a webcam/facetime, in your home or any location your child might be without you.

Be vigilant about pornography exposure.

Be sure you and your children know the laws about sexting and pornographic pictures. Kids often think the law is only for adults or that only their "friend" will see what they send.

LET'S LOOK AT JUST A FEW OF THE RISKS ASSOCIATED WITH YOU AND YOUR CHILD'S USE OF THE INTERNET

One in five U.S. teenagers who regularly log on to the Internet say they have received an unwanted sexual solicitation. Solicitations were defined as requests to engage in sexual activities or sexual talk, or to give personal sexual information (Oates, et al., 2000).

- 25% of children have been exposed to unwanted pornographic material online (Crimes Against Children Research Center).
- Only 1/3 of households with Internet access are actively protecting their children with filtering or blocking software (Crimes Against Children Research Center.)
- 75% of children are willing to share personal information online about themselves and their family in exchange for goods and services (eMarketer.)
- Only approximately 25% of children who encountered a sexual approach or solicitation told a parent or adult (Crimes Against Children Research Center.)
- One in 33 youth received an aggressive sexual solicitation in the past year. This means a predator asked a young person to meet somewhere, called a young person on the phone, and/or sent the young person correspondence, money, or gifts through the U.S. Postal Service (Youth Internet Safety Survey.)
- 77% of the targets for online predators were age 14 or older. Another 22% were users ages 10 to 13 (Crimes Against Children Research Center.)

3: SECURE IN YOUR SCHOOL

Like the other areas, basic SCHOOL SECURITY means you, as a parent, have to have regular involvement in order to keep your child safe. Because they will spend 25-50% of their waking hours in school, you want to be certain your school internet safety rules meet with your standard of safety. Additionally you want to review their child safety policies around child sexual abuse. If you work a full time job, you will still need to find ways and time to visit your child's school to make a personal assessment of the relationships between your child and the staff and parents who regularly interact with them. **Knowledge is key.**

- Know your child's primary school teachers, principals and other staff, coaches and other specialty leaders.
- Maintain a list of names, phone numbers and email addresses.
- Be certain you spend enough time at your child's school, for various functions and activities, you have personally observed faculty members' behaviors and attitude when interacting with your child.
- Keep lines of communication open, establishing regular dialogue with your child. Ask them how they feel about each adult or older juvenile they interact with at school.

- Talk to other parents if you see anything concerning regarding safety.
- Know the school's safety and security policies and ask them for a copy. If they do not have something in writing, insist it be put in writing. Facilitate any necessary changes. Angela's Voice has great resources for child safety policies that can be put in place in any organization working with children. They must include, but are not limited to detailed policy concerning the following:
  * One-adult-one-child interaction
  * One adult-one-juvenile interaction
  * Adult conduct guidelines
  * Sexual abuse prevention and detection methods
  * Child Sexual Abuse Disclosure Response plan

Be bold to confront school or program officials if policies need adjusting, or to express disagreement.

4: SECURE IN YOUR NEIGHBORHOOD AND 5: IN YOUR COMMUNITY

Finally, in the areas to secure, we will look at NEIGHBORHOOD and COMMUNITY. For the sake of simplicity, we define your NEIGHBORHOOD as any location within close proximity to your residence – a short walking distance. Your COMMUNITY can be any location your child spends time in, outside your home and beyond your neighborhood. This might be:

- Indoor and outdoor sports or recreational facilities
- Social and civic organizations.
- Homes well beyond the normal reach of your neighborhood, requiring transportation to arrive to and from.
- Churches and religious organizations.
- Youth serving organizations, such as Girl and Boy Scouts, volunteer events, social or educational clubs.
- Outings your child may take with various youth serving organizations.

NEIGHBORHOOD AND COMMUNITY SECURITY SHARE SOMETHING IN COMMON WITH SCHOOL SECURITY; THEY ARE BEYOND THE WATCHFUL EYE OF AN PARENT.

The further the distance your child is from home, the less likely you may be to participate or engage with your child in these locations, possibly putting them at greater risk. While we do not want to discourage activity outside the security of home, we do want to encourage security measures to reduce risks.

Take this opportunity to clearly express your expectations to your child and what is safe and unsafe best practices. It is never a best practice to be alone with an adult or older youth with the door closed. Your child may not instinctively know this fact.

- Establish a list of activities your child may engage in when they are not at home. Ask yourself what standard you want them to abide by when they are somewhere else. Have you communicated your safety rules regarding:

- Physical contact with other children or juveniles
- Physical contact with adults
- Sporting or play activities
- Movies or TV
- Reading materials
- Electronics or Internet access

Is your child allowed to engage in physical activities with other children, such as rough housing, hugging, wrestling, poking, touching? _____
_____

Is your child allowed to engage in physical contact with adults, such as hugging, piggy back rides, sitting on laps, full body contact, bathing, showering? _____
_____

Is your child allowed to watch any movie or television show outside your home? _____
_____

Is your child allowed access to view or read any materials they might come in contact with elsewhere, such as pornography, books with subject matters you disapprove of, certain comic books or magazines? _____
_____

Is your child allowed to access electronic games, cell phones for texting, Internet, or web cam when beyond your watchful eye? _____
_____

▶ Establish a list of locations your child is allowed to visit in your NEIGHBORHOOD and COMMUNITY
  * Outdoors
    - Yards, fields, parks in your immediate NEIGHBORHOOD
    - Recreation or sporting fields, basketball courts, tennis facilities, etc. in your COMMUNITY

  * Indoors
    - Homes – identify what portion of someone else's home they can be in – bedrooms, basements, living spaces, attics, etc.
    - Recreation facilities
    - Churches
    - Restaurants, theaters, retail locations, etc.

▶ Take the time to find out about these locations, who's in charge and what their particular standards and policies are regarding child-to-child interaction or child-to-adult interaction. Whether it's a neighbor's home, church, sports facility or other location, is there adult supervision? Get to know those people and what they allow when your child is under their authority. It can be especially easy to disregard this instruction when it comes to homes in your neighborhood. A parent can be fooled into a false sense of security because their child is in close physical proximity, but far too often it's in this false sense of security, where a child can be sexually abused.

POP IN UNANNOUNCED WHENEVER POSSIBLE

▸ For all COMMUNITY organizations and locations, maintain a file of their child sexual abuse safety and security policies. Ask the leadership for a physical copy. As a parent, you need to know what activities are allowed or disallowed between your child and other adults and/or juveniles. You should review these policies with your child. These policies should, at the very least, cover the following:
  * One-adult-one-child interaction
  * One-on-one juvenile (or child) interaction
  * Adult conduct guidelines
  * Sexual abuse prevention guidelines
  * Sexual abuse detection and disclosure methods

▸ Put together a clear and concise list of who you are allowing your child to spend time with outside your home. You need to KNOW these people.
  * Is there one or more persons 'in charge'? Who is he or she?
    - How do you maintain regular contact with them? Make sure you have address, phone and email on hand for each.
  * Limit or eliminate one-child-one-adult (or older juvenile) interaction for your child/ren.
    - This is where the risk of abuse is greatest.
  * Regularly check sex offender registries in the areas you live and play. They are available online through every municipal and county law enforcement agency.
    - **DO NOT RELY SOLELY ON THIS INFORMATION TO DETERMINE WHETHER SOMEONE IS SAFE FOR YOUR CHILD**
    - The 'average' sex offender will harm approximately 100+ children prior to being arrested the first time.

▸ Talk with your child. This cannot be stressed enough and should be part of each day. When you see your child, after they've been away from you, engage in conversation about what they did, who they were with and what they think of situations and people.

* Ask your child, frequently, how they feel about each adult or juvenile they interact with in the NEIGHBORHOOD and COMMUNITY. Be especially tuned in to any non-verbal communication or difficulty responding to questions. Validate any uneasiness they might feel and investigate personally.

▸ Be certain you spend enough time with your child's friends, in their homes and in the community locations where your child visits. Know who is present with your child.
* Observe the adult (or older juvenile) leaders' or parents' behavior and attitude, particularly toward your child.

When is the last time you asked your child how they feel about the people they interact with? _____

How often do you make surprise visits to homes, yards, recreation facilities? _____

Have you ever asked for a copy of safety and security policies from any organization your child is involved? _____

How much time, each week, does your child spend with people you don't know personally? _____

Your continued presence sends a message of security to your child and CAUTION to a POTENTIAL SEX OFFENDER! BE PRESENT!

Now that we've covered SECURING 5 AREAS, let's turn our focus to our 2 PRIMARY PEOPLE CONCERNS.

1: YOUR CHILD

This is the most significant portion of our lesson in Single Parenting Solutions – your child. Here, we give you information and tools to build upon your relationship with your child in an effort to affirm their value in the world and help keep them safe. More than anything else, how your child sees themselves in your family and in the world around them contributes greatly to their long-term emotional health. Your single most important job is to raise a child who is emotionally healthy, physically safe and secure in the love of family - in word and deed.

Encourage your child's SENSE OF VALUE

- Let your child be perfect just the way they are, without a bevy of unrealistic goals and expectations. Each of us has a unique identity and purpose in the world. We aren't raising 'mini mes'. We're raising individuals.
  * One of the challenges children in single parent households face most often is striving to be 'perfect'. In the shadow of an absentee parent, children can take on the idea they are somehow to blame for their family situation – defective in some way. Allowing your child the freedom to be imperfect and make mistakes gives them permission to let go of unnecessary burdens. A parenting style that includes consistency, approval, and acceptance can create positive self-esteem (Emler, 2002).

Does your child/ren take on unnecessary responsibility for any circumstances in your home? _____

If so, what? _____

How can you deter them from carrying the responsibility? _____
_____

Do you have unrealistic goals or expectations of your child? _____
_____

Do you expect them to be more like you, another sibling or family member? _____
_____

> How do you respond when your child makes mistakes? _____
> _____

- Love them for who they are. This falls in line with the previous concept. Don't compare your child to others in the family or in the world at large. If they are not as strong in areas of character or behavior as someone else, accept them. Validate their unique strengths and cover their weaknesses. That's what love does.

> Do you compare your child/ren to others? _____
> _____
> If so, who? _____
> _____
> Why? _____
> _____

Be particularly careful of comparing them to a person they know you do not like or to an ex-spouse or date.

- Honor their need for privacy or alone time. Let's agree from the start, privacy is NOT secrecy and it is up to you to determine which one your child is seeking at any given moment. Secrets can harm your child. Be sensitive and observe the time your child spends alone, honoring basic needs for privacy, while discouraging isolating and secretive behavior. The need for privacy is inherent in every individual and becomes more obvious as your child grows and matures. Some children have a greater need to unwind and be alone than others. Their home needs to be a sanctuary of peace and security, where they can spend whatever time is appropriate to their individual privacy needs. Anytime we do not honor another's heart and needs, we are potentially sending a message saying what we think or want is more important. This can cause children not to validate their own needs or trust their instincts.

Do you allow your child to be alone when they need to be? _____
_____

Can you tell the difference between your child/ren needing privacy and wanting to hide or isolate? _____
_____

Have you taught your child the difference between privacy and secrecy (or isolating)?
_____

- Identify their purpose (as is age appropriate). Just like you, your child will have different things that excite them throughout their maturing years. Building a strong foundation of value in them means affirming their passions. Remember, your child is not you. He or she is an individual, uniquely designed to accomplish different things in their life. Simple words of encouragement and regular affirmations send a message of validation to your child. In essence, you are saying, "I love that about you." Each of us needs validation, especially in areas where we feel most unlike the rest of the world. Find out what your child's passion is and support it 100%, through word and deed, even if it's short-lived.

List the names of each of your children and identify things that excite them, things they are passionate about:

NAME	PASSION	PASSION	PASSION

> Consider what you can do to affirm them in these areas. Can you get more involved? _____
> _____
> Be careful to allow them ownership. If they feel you "have" to be involved they may believe they cannot do it alone, losing enthusiasm and confidence.
> Do these things with them? _____
> Encourage your child to reach out to others with the same interest. Do you take your cues from your child? _____
> Are you available to help your child as they engage or learn about their passions? _____

- Allow them the full gamut of emotional expressions. All of us get sad, happy, angry, frustrated, anxious, etc. This includes our children. Each emotion, expressed appropriately, is valid and healthy. As a single parent, with much responsibility, it can be easy to curtail some emotional responses in our children. Let's face it, dealing with a child who is sad, angry or frustrated requires a lot of effort on a parent. It's one of the more challenging parts of the assignment. However, when a parent suppresses appropriate emotional responses in a children may learn to silence an integral part of themselves, believing it's either invalid or unwanted. This is a setup for failure long-term when they regress emotion. We should instill a sense of inner trust in our children. You want them to trust their instincts and boundaries, affirming them and teaching them to process each in ways that are healthy.

- Is there one or more emotional responses you find yourself wanting to suppress in your child/ren?

    ☐ ANGER   ☐ SADNESS   ☐ FRUSTRATION   ☐ JOY

    ☐ ANXIETY   ☐ WORRY   ☐ FEAR   ☐ EXUBERANCE

> What feelings arise in you when an unwanted emotional expression surfaces in your child? _____
>
> How do you normally respond to these unwanted emotional expressions? _____
>
> What message does your child/ren receive when you respond negatively in these situations? _____

Make a determination to help your child process his or her feelings appropriately. Step up to the plate and engage.

▸ Listen without distractions. It's an old adage "we have two ears and one mouth," but it bears repeating, especially in today's busy and technological lifestyle. Your children learn much of their value by the quality time and attention you are willing to give. It's not necessarily the amount of time you spend with them, but the undivided, affirming attention from you. Turn off the cell phone, Internet, television. Give your child the one-on-one time they need. Put a weekly 'date' on your calendar, one your child can look forward to, just the two of you.

Identify the last time you spent time with one or more children alone, face to face, without answering a phone, text, email, watching television, cooking, cleaning, knitting, etc. _____
How often would you say you disengage from distractions to give full attention to your child/ren? _____
Does one child get more undivided attention from you than the other/s? _____
If so, why? _____
What can you do to resolve any deficiencies in this area? _____

Remember, even if your child insists they don't need this time with you, they do! When a child balks at one-on-one time with a parent, it's often a result of our previous distracted interaction with them.

▸ Words of affirmation. Your child needs to hear you affirm them. As a parent, it is unwise to assume they 'know' how you feel about them. Words are powerful. They can help and heal or harm and hinder. The lack of words of affirmation can send negative messages: lack of concern, interest, validation, love. SPEAK! Your children are waiting.

Be careful to give meaningful praise. Kids are smart; they know when your praise is empty and just for show.

Make sure you tell your child frequently that you love them and you're glad they are in your life. Sometimes affirmation means saying some things like: "I am sorry, I have been short tempered with you; you don't deserve to be talked to in that manner. I am so glad you're in my life."

> Do you tell affirm your kids often enough? _____
>
> Do you need to apologize for your moods? _____

Catch your kids doing something good or fun and compliment them. You should give compliment 5 times more than you criticize. Comments like: You almost got it, try again", "I really see you trying, that is going to pay off," or "You're doing great, let me know if you want some help," all encourage and build up. Research shows that everyone, children in particular, responds better to praise than punishment and criticism.

- Physical contact with your child. Every human being needs healthy touch from others. Some research suggests we need 25 hugs daily to feel valued. Pat your child on the back. Hug them, even when they get old enough to resist out of embarrassment. Besides showing them you love them, this physical touch teaches an unspoken message about the difference between good touch and bad touch.

  When bankers train tellers to distinguish the authentic monetary bills from the counterfeits, they have them handle the 'real' stuff over and over again. The tellers become so comfortable with the feel of what's real, the incoming counterfeit is obvious. This is what you want to do as you engage in physical contact with your child. Teach them what 'real' and healthy relational contact looks like..

And, NEVER, cross your child's personal boundaries. Let your child determine what they want and don't want in terms of physical contact, whether it's with you, another relative, a friend, peer, or other adult. NEVER insist they kiss, hug, sit close to anyone they feel uncomfortable. Far too long we, as society, have delivered an unhealthy message to our children because of the desire to be 'nice' or 'courteous'. This insistence has contributed, in part, to our children not trusting their own instincts when something feels 'bad'.

Do you have physical contact with your child(ren) daily? _____

Do you know of any type of physical contact your child(ren) is uncomfortable with? Tickling? Pats on the head?_____

Have you ever instructed your child to kiss, hug or otherwise have physical contact with someone when they hesitated to do so? _____

- ▸ Pay attention to your child(ren). Involved parenting means you know your child(ren). While it may seem a simple concept, it can get lost in the hustle of everyday life. Take notice of your child's moods, behaviors, patterns, habits, relationships, likes and dislikes.

- ▸ Set healthy limits for your child(ren). All children need boundaries. Like backyard fences, boundaries are designed to keep one inside in safety, free to roam and be themselves. Ideally, you want to set healthy boundaries while affording your child the opportunity to take age appropriate risks. By doing so, you allow your child to make decisions, step out of their comfort zone and see what results. This is one of the best ways to teach your child to trust their own decision-making abilities. Whether it's riding their bike a little further down the driveway, learning to rock climb, or standing on stage in a play, age appropriate risks build self-esteem. Find ways to let your child take risks.

- ▸ Affirm the very important lesson of making mistakes. Let your child know everyone makes mistakes and they are vital to our development. Mistakes provide a myriad of healthy lessons in decision-making, instincts, humility, response to failure – all potentially valuable and healthy when given the freedom to make and process them. Determine to de-mystify mistakes. Don't condemn or over-react when your child makes mistakes. Engage in discussion, help them process and move on with encouragement.

How do you respond when your child(ren) makes a mistake? _____
_____

Do you take it personally, believing it reflects on you as a parent? _____

How does your child perceive his or her mistakes? _____
Are they afraid to admit they've failed? _____
Does he or she fear your reaction? _____

- Make sure your child has a place of comfort and emotional safety inside the family and home. The outside world can be full of demands, expectations, difficulties and pressures for your child. Home should be their safe place to be themselves. Let them. Let them know they are free to be safe and loved inside the family – where your acceptance, forgiveness and encouragement are always available to them.

- Let your child VENT. Often the world hurts, frustrates or just makes us mad. Allow your child to vent and express these emotions. These emotions don't feel good, but having them is ok. Teach your child that you will listen to them and help them figure out what to do with their emotions. Sometimes just expressing the feel bad emotions allow us to move on. This also shows your child that you can handle the "hard and bad stuff;" that you can be trusted to hear anything.

TRUSTING THEIR INNER VOICE

- MODEL this behavior for your child. One of the ways your child learns throughout life is by watching you model behaviors. In the case of trusting their INNER VOICE, or instinct, is for you to let them see you trust yours. How does this play out in day to day life? All too often, we can keep things hidden from our children. Many adult matters are best kept for adults. But, certain situations do present teahable moments for your child. On a daily basis, a parent can face decisions requiring one's instinct. Do I do this event or that? Do I travel this road or that one? Sometimes we run into a circumstance or person causing our 'red flag' to be raised. This is the perfect time to model and discuss with your child the need to change directions or heed a 'red flag' even when you are unsure the cause.

- All children have an inherent INNER VOICE. As a parent, you see this early on in children. Your toddler does not like a person, dog, food, or location. They become hot, cold, hungry, or uncomfortable. Even before they are able to communicate verbally, they send cues expressing their likes and dislikes. These are early examples of an inherent INNER VOICE and personal boundaries.

Can you remember any time/s when your child didn't feel 'right' about something? _____
_____

How did they express this? _____

How did you respond? _____

Your child's responses to their INNER VOICE may show up differently as they grow. Watch for their cues. Your child may tell you something just feels 'good' or another thing feels 'bad.' He or she may have a facial or other physical reaction. When you hear or see this in your child, engage in a conversation. Find out what they feel and think. Stop and listen. When learning to honor their own INNER VOICE, your child may find words challenging. Give them time to process verbally, without interruption. And, above all, AFFIRM them. Whether you think or feel the same way, give them credit for trusting themselves.

▶ Don't disregard your child. In the course of the day, it can be easy to disregard your child or ignore them. Parents can say things to their child like, "Oh, honey, it's no big deal", "Not now" or "Let it go" in response to their sharing something important to them. Again, it can't be said enough, anytime a parent silences a child, it can send a small part of them into hiding. Parents don't usually do so intentionally, but children perceive it as if it were. It only takes a minute or two to affirm your child.

Have you ever glossed over something your child tries to talk with you about because you're too busy? _____
How does your child respond when you send the message you don't have time or energy for what they're sharing with you? _____
_____
_____

What steps can you take, today, to actively listen to your child/ren more? _____
_____
_____

- Develop guidelines for safety around your child's natural instincts. Confirming your child's instincts comes first, but must be followed with instruction for how to behave when a 'red flag' goes off. Use each opportunity to train them in an age appropriate manner. When something feels 'off' to them, ask questions and listen for their answers. Once your child begins to process his or her feelings, you may begin to ask them how they would like to handle the situation. Children are often surprisingly wise when trusting their instincts. When need be, offer up suggestions while affirming their position and feelings.

> If your child is with another person and feels uncomfortable, what do you want them to do? _____
> _____
>
> If your child sees or hears something they sense is wrong, how do you want them to proceed? _____
> _____

Use your child's regular interactions with others to discuss 'what ifs'. Role play their possible responses. Write them down and practice, as is age appropriate.

- Teach your child it's OK to say "NO" to someone or something that doesn't feel 'right' to them. This is another area where we, as a society at large, have failed our children. No parent really wants their child to come across as negative or rebellious, yet there are times when this response to a person or situation is justified. Parents, as you encourage your child to trust his or her instincts, be sure to follow up with a clear teaching about saying "NO" to ANYONE or ANYTHING that makes them uncomfortable. If and when this would happen, be sure your first response to the incident is to stand in defense of your child's actions. You can iron out details later, but the first thing your child and their offender need to see and hear is your affirmation!

Teach at every age

EQUIPPED TO BE SAFE AND SECURE

Let's review what your child needs in order feel Safe and Secure

- Meet their basic physical needs. Make sure they have food, water and shelter. If you ever require assistance to meet these needs, reach out for help in your community. Keep your home as orderly as possible. An organized home creates a more secure environment for your child.

- Provide PHYSICAL and EMOTIONAL safety. Raise them in a home free of physical and sexual abuse. Safeguard them with systems and deterrents included in this workbook. Abstain from psychological and emotional abuse. Single parenting is tough. Be good to yourself. Lower your stress as well as your high expectations for your children's behavior. Find resources to help you manage, should you find yourself wanting to verbally or emotionally harm your child.

- Love in ACTION. Your child needs to see and feel your love, by your actions, all of them. Love them in word, deed, touch, availability. Your love needs to be secure, stable and consistent.

- Reward TRUTH and discourage SECRETS. Establish a 'NO SECRETS' policy with your child/ren. Encourage them to share everything with you and make sure you are available so they can. Praise your child for telling you the truth, especially if they face discipline for coming forward. This will secure in their hearts what you've said with your mouth – tell everything.

- Be a place of COMFORT. Design your family and home to be a place of comfort and security for your child to be his or her authentic self.

- Parental INVOLVEMENT. We live in a busy world. Single parents can find it's even more true for themselves. No matter how busy your schedule is, carve out time to participate in your child's life. Drop other less important things. Schedule yourself into your child's life.

Encourage the non-custodial parent to be equally involved with your child. Your child loves you both, equally, regardless of circumstances or hurts. They need you both. Be active in encouraging that relationship. It's for your child's healthy future.

- Be a responsible, HEALTHY PARENT. Parenting isn't for lightweights. It's work. Lead by example. Keep yourself emotionally and physically healthy. Keep your child protected from adult matters. Let him or her be a CHILD.
- Find ways to HAVE FUN!! Children need to play – with you and with their friends. Let them! Encourage relationships with friends and find ways to interact and play with them yourself. Friendly play recharges your child's batteries. Family play and laughter is rewarding and builds intimate bonds.

WHO WILL BE WITH YOUR CHILD?

Ask these questions about each and every older juvenile and adult your child will interact with:

- How well do I know them?
- How long have I known them?
- How much personal information do I have on them?
- Address, phone, email, occupation, family status.
- What kind of physical and emotional contact does my child have with them?
- How does my child feel about them? Behave after being with them?
- Is my child ever alone with them? For how long and where?
- Have I stopped in unexpectedly when they are with my child?
- Have I ruled out any criminal history?
- Have you consistently reviewed sex offender registries in your area?

Being FREE of a criminal record does NOT mean someone is 'SAFE' for your child!

As a single parent we applaud your efforts to get trained and educated on how you can better protect your child against the risk of child sexual abuse. We hope you find the training in Single Parent Solutions helpful in predicting and preventing child sexual abuse in your home and community. Please share the information you have learned and feel free to contact Angela's Voice and visit **angelasvoice.com** for additional awareness, prevention and healing programs and resources.

REFERENCES

Bourland, J. (Dec 2000/Jan 2001) When the child is the parent. *Parenting* Vol. 14, Iss. 10. Page 258.

Bromfield, R. (Feb/Mar 2008). On your own. *Scholastic Parent & Child.* Vol. 15, Iss. 5. Page 56. Feb/Mar 2008.)

Centers for Disease Control and Prevention, National Center for Injury Prevention and Control, Division of Violence Prevention. Adverse Childhood Experiences (ACE) Study. Retrieved from: http://www.cdc.gov/nccdphp/ace/findings.htm

Chicago Crime Commission Report. (1995). Children in need: Investment strategies. Committee for Economic Development.

Children's Defense Fund. (1998). The state of America's children, 1998 Yearbook.

Children's Defense Fund Annual Report 2011.

Dush, Clair Kamp. (2009). Family stability may be more crucial than two parents for child success. *Research.* http://researchnews.osu.edu/archive/familystability.htm

Emler, N. (2002). The costs and causes of low self-esteem. Youth Studies Australia, 21(3), 45.

eMarketer

FBI Law Enforcement Bulletin - Investigative Aid

Furstenberg, F., Cherlin, A. (1991). Divided families. Harvard University.

Gomes-Schwartz , B., Horowitz, J, & Cardarelli, A. P. (July 1988). Child Sexual Abuse Victims and Their Treatment. U.S. Department of Justice, Office of Juvenile Justice and Delinquency Prevention. Washington D.C. Print.

Hughes, R., Jr. (2005). The effects of divorce on children. Urbana, IL: University of Illinois Extension. Retrieved from: http://parenting247.org/article.cfm?ContentID=646

Kelly, J. & Wallerstein, J. (1980).Surviving the breakup. (p.125). NY: Basic Books: Print.

Koch. M. P., & Lowery, C.R. (1984). Visitation and the noncustodial father. *Journal of Divorce and Remarriage*, Vol. 8(2), 50.

MacLanahan, S. S. & Sandefur, G. (1994). *Growing up with a single parent: What hurts, what helps.* Cambridge, MA: Harvard University Press.

Metzler, C. W.; Noell, J.; Biglan, A.; Ary, D.; Smolkowski, K. (August 1994).The social context for risky sexual behavior among adolescents. *Journal of Behavioral Medicine*, Vol 17(4), Aug, 419-438. doi:10.1007/BF01858012

National Center for Health Statistics

National Mental Health Association

National Center for Missing and Exploited Children. (2006).

National Commission on Children. (1991). Speaking of kids.

Oates, R. K., D.P. Jones, D. Denson, A. Sirotnak, N. Gary, and R.D. Krugman. (200). Erroneous concerns about child sexual abuse. *Child Abuse & Neglect* 24:149-57. Print.

Parents Without Partners

Parke, Mary. (May 2003). Are married parents really better for children? What research says about the effects of family structure on child well-being. *CLASP, Couples and Marriage Series.* Retrieved from: http://www.clasp.org/admin/site/publications_archive/files/0128.pdf

Solo Parenting Alliance

Sommer, R. (2004). Parent alienation syndrome: A war children cannot win. Parent Rise. Retrieved from http://www.parentrise.com/counseling/war-children-cannot-win.html

U.S. Census Department. (2007).

U.S. Department of Health and Human Services. (1993). National Center for Health Statistics, Survey of Child Health. Government Printing Office: Washington, D. C. Print.

Wolak, J., Finkelhor, D., & Mitchell, K. (Dec 2007). Fact Sheet: 1 in 7 youth: The statistics about online sexual solicitations. University of New Hampshire, Crimes against Children Research Center. Retrieved from: http://www.unh.edu/ccrc/internet-crimes/factsheet_1in7.html

Wolf, J. Single Parent Statistics. About.com. Retrieved from: www.singleparents.about.com/od/legalissues/p/portrait.htm

Youth Internet Safety Survey

SINGLE PARENTING 53

EQUIPPED TO
QUICK REFERENCE GUIDE FOR PARENTS

PARENTING BE'S

BE FOCUSED and PRESENT in your child's life

- **Physically** – spend quality time together. Cuddle, talk, do activities.
- **Mentally** – Engage them. Talk about things your child gets excited about.
- **Emotionally** – Listen to your child and let them talk. Your child feels emotionally connected when you listen. Be available for their emotional needs, even when they aren't verbalizing them.
- **Undivided attention** – without distractions, interruptions or multi-tasking

BE FLEXIBLE with your child's needs

- **NEEDS** arise suddenly sometimes – prepare for them and make concessions in your plans or routine when they do
- **Stay 'IN THE MOMENT'** – Stop what you're doing to connect with your child when he or she needs you.

BE DILIGENT to show how much you value your child

- **Ensuring your child THRIVES** means your actions and words must be consistent throughout their days, months and years.

BE DETERMINED to be the parent your child deserves!

"A well-attended child is like a well-watered garden."

ANGELA'S VOICE

Angela's Voice is dedicated to developing, distributing, and endorsing valuable resources in the awareness, prevention, and healing of child sexual abuse. The materials, though specific for survivors of child sexual abuse, also benefit any abuse survivor and help protect children by teaching them how to defend themselves from abusive behavior. Founder Angela Williams, MFP, is a survivor-turned-advocate who shares a powerful message of triumph over tragedy by sharing her vulnerable and candid voice about her abuse trauma, her pain, her struggles, and her journey to healing in hopes that it may help other survivors expedite their healing journey.

Williams has devoted years to providing awareness, prevention, and healing programs through her advocacy work. Williams has captivated audiences with her powerful message of triumph over tragedy as a victim of childhood physical and sexual abuse. At age seventeen, she attempted suicide, and that day was the end of her torment and the beginning of a journey to healing. She is a crusader for change and dedicates her life to eradicate child sexual abuse. She holds a master's in forensic psychology with a concentration in child abuse. Williams is a powerful messenger, appearing in national and international news and documentaries. She has been successful in state legislative reform and national policy work and served on the Policy Committee of the National Coalition to Prevent Child Sexual Abuse and Exploitation. She has received numerous accolades and awards for her work, including her collection of books that have valuable lessons for survivors of all ages.

Please follow Angela Williams on social media and contact angelasvoice.com

to book a speaking event or interview.

Books by Angela Williams

Loving Me: After Abuse
From Sorrows to Sapphires, Angela Williams's Memoir

Interactive Workbooks—Adults

Healing

Pathway to Healing, Guide to Healing
True Intimacy
Shattering the Shame
Unveiling Child Sexual Abuse

Prevention

Tough Talk to Tender Hearts
The Grooming Mystery
Single Parenting Solutions
Courage to Speak

Children's Books (Ages 5–10)

Gracie Finds Her Voice
Grant Gets His Shield
Gracie and Grant's Big Win
Gracie and Grant's Big Win Coloring Book
Find Your Voice Curriculum Book

Join the Angela's Voice Movement

Take action to break the silence and cycle of Child Sexual Abuse and Exploitation

HELP US SAVE THE NEXT GENERATION OF CHILDREN!

1. Be a Child Advocate
2. Donate at angelasvoice.com
3. Invite Angela Williams to Speak
4. Purchase another Angela's Voice Prevention or Healing Book

Discover more child sexual abuse prevention and healing resources at **angelasvoice.com** and follow angelasvoice in social media.

Instagram @Angelasvoice

Facebook @Angelasvoice

Twitter @Angelasvoice

Linkedin/angelasvoice

Angelasvoice.blogspot.com

Youtube.com/angelakwilliams

www.ingramcontent.com/pod-product-compliance
Lightning Source LLC
Chambersburg PA
CBHW040010080526
44586CB00028B/2949